Flower Shop

Eira Reeves

Duncan, Flora and Fred the dog all worked in a flower shop.

When customers came into the shop they always gave Fred a pat.

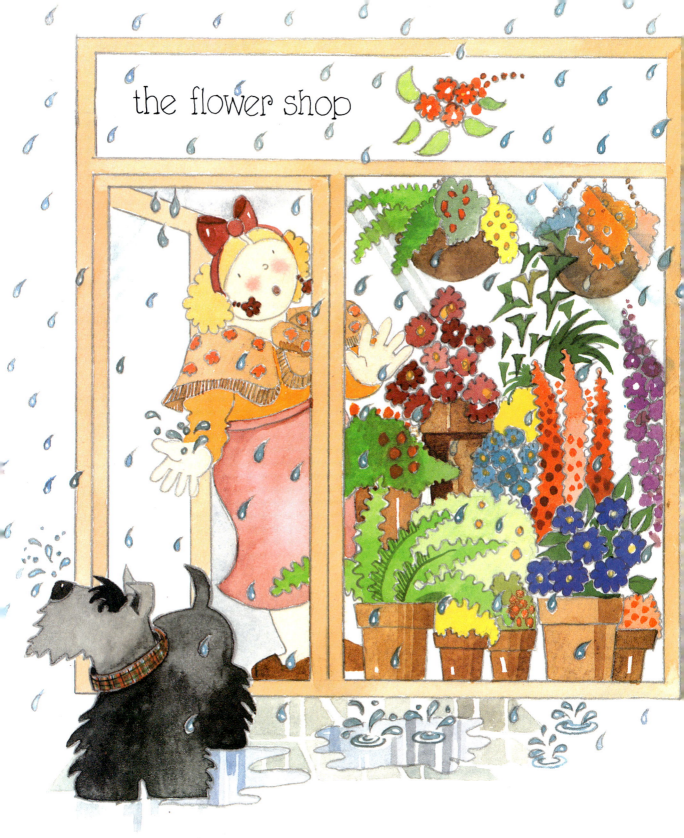

But one Wednesday morning it was raining.
"Oh dear, there won't be many customers today," Flora said.

Fred felt gloomy too. He wouldn't get many pats today either.

Then Flora had an idea.
"I'll put Fred in the window so he can look out," she said.
Fred felt happier.

He looked out at one little passer-by,
and decided to do one of his tricks.

He sat up and begged.

The little passer-by was joined by her brother and they began to laugh at Fred.

Fred rolled over and did another trick.

More passers-by stopped to look. They laughed at Fred too.

Gradually a crowd gathered. Everyone was laughing at Fred.

Flora and Duncan enjoyed Fred's tricks too!

People came into the shop to thank Fred for cheering them up on such a rainy day. They bought bunches and bunches of flowers and gave Fred lots of pats.

At the end of the day the shop was empty.
All the flowers had been sold. Flora and Duncan were delighted.

And so was Fred!